THE ZERO OF LIFE

YASHI K

To those who have ever felt unseen, unheard, or forgotten. This is for the ones who have lived in the shadow of silence, but found their way toward the light. I dedicate this to those who have been called "zero" but are everything and more.

Contents

FOREWORD

In this story, you will encounter the raw and unfiltered emotions of a person who grew up carrying the weight of rejection and isolation. It's not an easy journey to follow, but it is a necessary one. Many have experienced moments of self-doubt and defeat, but few have the courage to document the painful road back to self-discovery and healing.

This book is not just a story of personal growth; it is a message to anyone who has ever felt like they were not enough. It's a reminder that the human spirit, though bruised and battered, can rise again. The author's vulnerability will inspire you to reconsider what it means to start over and to redefine your own narrative, regardless of the labels others might try to impose on you.

PREFACE

This book was born from years of silence—years spent believing that I was worth nothing. But through that silence, I found my voice. Writing became my way of processing the world around me, even when the world refused to acknowledge my existence.

For many years, I thought I was alone in my struggle, and maybe you feel that way too. This book is not just my story—it is a testimony to everyone who has faced rejection, mockery, or isolation. It's a reflection of the quiet battles we fight within ourselves and a reminder that even the smallest flicker of hope can light a path forward.

I hope that in sharing my journey, others might find comfort, validation, and perhaps, a little piece of themselves in these pages.

ACKNOWLEDGEMENTS

This book would not have been possible without the support and encouragement of several individuals.

To my parents, who gave me the strength to keep moving forward, even when I felt like standing still.

To the few friends who believed in me when I couldn't believe in myself—thank you for seeing me when I felt invisible.

To the teachers and mentors who taught me, directly or indirectly, that my value cannot be measured by others' opinions. Your words, both harsh and kind, have shaped my journey in more ways than you know.

Lastly, to every reader who has ever struggled with their sense of worth—this story is for you. Thank you for being part of this journey with me.

I used to believe that life was about numbers. Grades, scores, rankings—they all seemed to define who I was and what I would become. But then came the number zero, a symbol that haunted me through childhood and adolescence. It was the number that followed me like a shadow, whispered in the hallways, written on the report cards, and stamped into my identity.

Zero was not just a number. It was a label, a verdict passed down by those around me. It was a reminder that, no matter how hard I tried, I would always be less than—always be nothing.

But what if zero wasn't the end? What if it was a beginning?

This story is my search for an answer to that question. It's the tale of how I began as nothing, but learned that being nothing gave me the space to become anything. This is the journey of how zero, once a curse, became my opportunity to redefine who I am...

I

THE BEGINNING OF SILENCE

I was seven when I first realized that I was different. Not in the way that you see in movies, where being different leads to some extraordinary fate. My difference was quiet, invisible, and isolating. I sat on the last bench in school, always observing but never part of the conversation. The other kids laughed, shared jokes, and passed notes. But for me, there was only silence.

It wasn't always like that. In the beginning, I was just another child in the classroom, trying to find my place. But then, it started. The looks.

The whispers. And then the teacher's words, sharper than any whisper, cutting through the air and through me. "You're a zero. No matter how hard you try, zero times a hundred is still zero. That's what you'll always be—nothing."

II

THE STING OF WORDS

At first, I didn't understand what it meant. Zero? Why was I a zero? But the more I heard it, the more I believed it. My classmates began to distance themselves. "Don't talk to her," they'd say, "or you'll become a zero too." Those words spread like wildfire. My name became a ghost in the school, replaced by a single number: zero.

Every day, I'd sit in class, pretending not to hear their words. Pretending that the sting didn't reach me. But inside, I was drowning in it. It was as if the whole world had turned against me. I tried to focus on my studies, tried to raise my hand to answer questions, but the teacher would ignore me. Her gaze would pass over me *as if I didn't exist.*

III

THE WEIGHT OF LONELINESS

The loneliness began to weigh heavier with each passing day. It wasn't just the isolation from my classmates that hurt—it was the isolation from the world. The teacher's words echoed in my head, and no matter how hard I tried to forget, they stayed with me. I could see the pity in the eyes of the students who sat at the front, the smirks on the faces of those in the middle rows.

I became invisible. And being invisible is the worst kind of pain. You don't exist in the minds of others. You're a shadow. A shadow that no one cares to look at or acknowledge. I was reduced to a number—zero. And I started to believe that maybe I was worth nothing, after all.

IV
THE FALL

By the time I reached high school, my confidence was shattered. The words had taken root deep inside me. No one spoke to me anymore, and even if they did, it was with mockery or disdain. The teachers, once my guides, had become my biggest critics. They no longer bothered with encouragement or correction. "You'll never make it," one of them said, shaking her head as if I had already failed. "A zero always remains a zero."

With each passing year, the burden grew heavier. I stopped trying. What was the point? If the world already saw me as a failure, why fight it? I stopped raising my hand. I stopped attempting to make friends. I became the last bench occupant who was easy to forget, and soon, even easier to ignore.

V

THE FINAL BLOW

When 12th grade came to an end, I felt a tiny spark of hope. Maybe this chapter of my life would close, and I could start fresh somewhere else. Maybe, in a new place, I wouldn't be a zero. Maybe I could be something more.

But when the rejections started rolling in, one after another, that spark was extinguished. No university wanted me. "We regret to inform you..." "Your application has not been successful..." The words blurred together until they all sounded the same: you're not good enough. You're nothing. Zero.

I was crushed. All the hope I had built up over the years, the tiny pieces of it that I had clung to, crumbled into dust. It felt like the world was confirming what I had feared all along—that I was destined to be nothing.

•

VI

THE FOUR YEARS OF SILENCE

It's been four years since that day. Four years of living in the shadows of my own home, confined within the walls of my room. The outside world moved on without me. My parents stopped asking about my plans. I stopped pretending to have any.

For four years, I've woken up each day, gone through the motions of life, but not really living. My existence has become a cycle of pretending—pretending that I'm fine, pretending that the rejections didn't destroy me, pretending that I still believe there's a future out there for me.

But deep down, I know the truth. I am a zero. And maybe I've always been a zero. I can't shake the feeling that I've been living under this label for so long that it's become a part of me. The longer I stay trapped in this silence, the more I believe it.

VII
THE QUESTION

One night, when everything was still and the world seemed to be sleeping, a question came to me. It was quiet at first, like a whisper at the back of my mind, but it grew louder until it was impossible to ignore.

"Am I really destined to remain a zero?"

It seemed like such a simple question, but it carried the weight of everything I had been through. The years of isolation, the rejection, the self-doubt—all of it hung on that one question. Was this really all I was meant to be? Was there no escape from the shadow of zero?

I didn't know the answer. But the fact that the question had even crossed my mind was enough to stir something inside me. A flicker, a tiny spark that I hadn't felt in years. What if zero wasn't the end? What if zero was just the beginning?

VIII

THE FLICKER OF HOPE

The next day, that question lingered in my mind. It was a strange feeling, carrying hope again, even if it was small and fragile. I began to think about what zero really meant. Was it truly the end? Or was it a blank slate, a starting point?

I had always seen zero as nothing, as emptiness, but what if it was space? Space to grow, to begin again? It seemed impossible to change my life after so many years of feeling lost, but maybe that's exactly what I needed to do.

I started small. I picked up old hobbies that I had abandoned years ago. I began writing again, putting my thoughts onto paper, even if they were messy and unclear. I read books that inspired me, books that made me think that maybe, just maybe, I wasn't as alone as I thought.

IX

THE PATH FARWARD

Slowly, I started to feel like there was a path ahead of me, even if it was still hidden in the shadows. It wasn't easy, and there were days when the weight of the past felt too heavy to carry. But each day, I reminded myself that I wasn't bound by what others had called me. Zero didn't define me. It was just a part of my story, not the whole story.

I started reaching out to people, joining online courses, and applying to universities again. It was terrifying—putting myself out there after so many years of rejection—but something had shifted. I wasn't as afraid of failure anymore because I had lived with it for so long. I knew it couldn't break me any more than it already had.

long. I knew it couldn't break me any more than it already had.

X

BECOMING SOMETHING MORE

Months passed, and slowly, doors began to open. Small successes started to pile up. An acceptance letter came through. Then another. Each one felt like a piece of my life falling back into place, but this time, it was different. This time, I wasn't chasing perfection. I wasn't afraid of being a zero anymore.

Because I had learned something through all the years of silence and rejection: zero is where you start. It's where you have the freedom to become anything, to rewrite your story. And for the first time in my life, I realized that being a zero wasn't the end—it was the beginning of everything.

being a zero wasn't the end—it was the beginning of everything.

Epilogue

As I write these final words, I realize that this journey is far from over. The process of healing, of growing, of becoming more than the labels I've carried will continue. But I no longer fear the future, nor do I dread the unknown. Instead, I embrace it. Zero, once a symbol of emptiness, has become a space of infinite possibility.

This story is just one chapter in the ongoing journey of my life, and I hope it serves as a reminder that it's never too late to rewrite your own narrative. If you've ever felt like a zero, know that you have the power to redefine yourself, to start over, and to become something greater than you ever imagined.

Afterword

Looking back on my journey, it's hard to believe how far I've come. What began as a story of pain and isolation has transformed into one of resilience and hope. Writing this book has been both difficult and cathartic, but it has allowed me to process emotions that I kept buried for so long.

I hope that by sharing my experiences, I've been able to connect with others who have faced similar struggles. Life doesn't come with a set path, and sometimes we find ourselves lost in the silence of rejection. But I've learned that it's in those quiet moments that we discover who we truly are.

GRATITUDE

As I conclude this book, I realize that no journey is ever truly walked alone. Even in moments of isolation, there are people who offer their quiet support, their unwavering belief, or simply their presence. I want to acknowledge those who have stood by me, whether they knew it or not.

To my parents, for your patience and quiet encouragement during the most difficult years. Even when words were few, your love was constant, and that gave me the strength to keep going.

To the friends who stayed, even when I had nothing to give. Your presence, even in the smallest of gestures, reminded me that I was not alone.

To the readers—thank you for taking the time to step into my story. Whether this book reflects your own experience or offers a new perspective, I hope it has been meaningful in some way. Your support means more to me than you may ever know.

Lastly, I acknowledge myself. For every day I chose to keep going, for every moment I fought to find hope. This book is proof that, no matter how dark the journey, there is always light ahead.

AUHTOR'S NOTE

Thank you for reading The Zero of Life. This story was incredibly personal, and putting it into words was one of the hardest things I've ever done. But if sharing my journey helps even one person feel less alone or more hopeful, then it has been worth every moment.

If this book resonated with you, or if you want to share your own story, I encourage you to reach out. Life can feel overwhelming at times, but when we open up, we realize that we're not walking through it alone.